W9-BSL-336

OCT   2007

The · Life Cycle · Series

The Life Cycle of an

Emperor Penguin

Bobbie Kalman & Robin Johnson

Crabtree Publishing Company

www.crabtreebooks.com

The Life Cycle Series
A Bobbie Kalman Book

Dedicated by Margaret Amy Salter
To John Reynolds — the only man I know who has his own penguin suit!

Editor-in-Chief
Bobbie Kalman

Writing team
Bobbie Kalman
Robin Johnson

Substantive editors
Kelley MacAulay
Kathryn Smithyman

Project editor
Michael Hodge

Editors
Molly Aloian
Rebecca Sjonger

Design
Margaret Amy Salter
Samantha Crabtree (cover)

Production coordinator
Heather Fitzpatrick

Photo research
Crystal Foxton

Consultant
Patricia Loesche, Ph.D., Animal Behavior Program,
Department of Psychology, University of Washington

Illustrations
Barbara Bedell: page 10
Katherine Kantor: page 26 (bottom)
Vanessa Parson-Robbs: pages 5 (middle), 9 (feathers), 11 (fledgling), 21 (bottom), 26 (top)
Margaret Amy Salter: back cover, pages 4, 5 (left and right), 8, 9 (magnifying glass),
    11 (all except fledgling), 21 (top), 30, 31

Photographs
Kevin Schafer/Peter Arnold/Alpha Presse: pages 14, 15
Animals Animals - Earth Scenes: © OSF/Allan, Doug: page 7; © Bedell, Daniel A.:
    title page; © Kooyman, Gerald L.: pages 9, 13, 25 (top); © Lister/OSF: page 30
ardea.com: Graham Robertson: page 16
© Wolfgang Kaehler, www.wkaehlerphoto.com: pages 5, 22
Minden Pictures: Pete Oxford: page 25 (bottom); Tui De Roy: page 12
Naturepl.com: Doug Allan: pages 17, 18, 27; Martha Holmes: page 26
Photo Researchers, Inc.: Kevin Schafer: page 19; Art Wolfe: page 20
SeaPics.com: © Bryan & Cherry Alexander: page 31; © Mark Jones: page 10;
    © Fritz Poelking/V&W: page 23
Other images by Digital Stock and Digital Vision

Library and Archives Canada Cataloguing in Publication

Kalman, Bobbie, date.
    The life cycle of an emperor penguin / Bobbie Kalman & Robin Johnson.

(The life cycle series)
Includes index.
ISBN-13: 978-0-7787-0630-4 (bound)
ISBN-10: 0-7787-0630-3 (bound)
ISBN-13: 978-0-7787-0704-2 (pbk.)
ISBN-10: 0-7787-0704-0 (pbk.)
    1. Emperor penguin--Life cycles--Juvenile literature. I. Johnson,
Robin (Robin R.) II. Title. III. Series: Life cycle

QL696.S473K34 2006   j598.47   C2006-904094-X

Library of Congress Cataloging-in-Publication Data

Kalman, Bobbie.
    The life cycle of an emperor penguin / Bobbie Kalman & Robin Johnson.
        p. cm. -- (The life cycle series)
Includes index.
ISBN-13: 978-0-7787-0630-4 (rlb)
ISBN-10: 0-7787-0630-3 (rlb)
ISBN-13: 978-0-7787-0704-2 (pb)
ISBN-10: 0-7787-0704-0 (pb)
    1. Emperor penguin--Life cycles--Antarctica--Juvenile literature. I. Johnson,
Robin (Robin R.) II. Title. II. Series.

QL696.S473K33 2007
598.47--dc22

                                        2006018781
                                        LC

Crabtree Publishing Company

www.crabtreebooks.com   1-800-387-7650

Copyright © **2007 CRABTREE PUBLISHING COMPANY**. All rights reserved. No part of this publication may be reproduced, stored in a retrieval system or be transmitted in any form or by any means, electronic, mechanical, photocopying, recording, or otherwise, without the prior written permission of Crabtree Publishing Company. In Canada: We acknowledge the financial support of the Government of Canada through the Book Publishing Industry Development Program (BPIDP) for our publishing activities.

Published in Canada
Crabtree Publishing
616 Welland Ave.
St. Catharines, ON
L2M 5V6

Published in the United States
Crabtree Publishing
PMB16A
350 Fifth Ave., Suite 3308
New York, NY 10118

Published in the United Kingdom
Crabtree Publishing
White Cross Mills
High Town, Lancaster
LA1 4XS

Published in Australia
Crabtree Publishing
386 Mt. Alexander Rd.
Ascot Vale (Melbourne)
VIC 3032

Contents

What is a penguin?   4

The coldest place on Earth   6

An emperor penguin's body   8

What is a life cycle?   10

Journey on the ice   12

Penguin partners   14

The emperors and the eggs   16

The chicks hatch   18

Chick care   20

Growing in a group   22

Mature penguins   24

Life in the ocean   27

Long live the emperors!   28

People and penguins   30

Glossary and Index   32

What is a penguin?

A penguin is a **bird**. A bird is an animal that has feathers, a beak, two legs, and two wings. Unlike most birds, penguins do not use their wings to fly. Penguins live mainly in water, so they use their wings to swim. Like all birds, penguins breathe air using **lungs**. Lungs are body parts that take in and let out air. Penguins cannot breathe under water. They must swim to the surface of the water to breathe air.

Warm blooded

A penguin is a **warm-blooded** animal. The body temperature of a warm-blooded animal stays about the same in both cold and warm places. Most penguins live in places that are very cold. Their thick feathers help keep them warm.

Emperor penguins are large penguins. They stand about 45 inches (114 cm) tall and weigh between 48 and 81 pounds (22-37 kg).

Penguin colonies

There are 17 **species**, or types, of penguins. This book is about emperor penguins. Like all penguins, emperor penguins live in groups called **colonies**, such as the one shown right. Emperor penguins travel, raise their babies, and hunt for food in colonies.

The macaroni penguin is a crested penguin. Crested penguins have feathers sticking out of the tops of their heads.

Little blue penguins are the smallest species of penguins. They are the size of ducks.

Adélie penguins are the most common species of penguins.

The coldest place on Earth

A **habitat** is the natural place where an animal lives. An emperor penguin's habitat is the Southern Ocean. The Southern Ocean surrounds Antarctica. Antarctica is the most southern **continent** and the coldest place on Earth. The Southern Ocean is so cold that the surface freezes into large pieces of ice. These huge blocks of floating ice are called **pack ice**. When emperor penguins leave the water, they often move onto pack ice.

Emperor penguins spend most of their time swimming in the Southern Ocean.

Light or dark

Antarctica is in the **Southern Hemisphere**. In most of the Southern Hemisphere, there are four seasons: spring, summer, autumn, and winter. In Antarctica, there are only two seasons, however: a cold summer and a freezing winter. During summer, the sun shines almost all day long. During winter, it is dark nearly 24 hours a day.

Freezing temperatures

When emperor penguins are out of the ocean, they are in the coldest, windiest, and driest **climate** in the world. The average temperature in Antarctica is about -58° F (-50° C)! In winter, there are powerful storms and freezing winds that blow up to 200 miles (322 km) per hour! Antarctica is covered in snow all year. It receives less than two inches (5 cm) of **precipitation** each year, but the temperature never gets warm enough in Antarctica to melt all the snow.

There are about 40 colonies of emperor penguins in Antarctica.

An emperor penguin's body

The body of an emperor penguin is designed for life in the Southern Ocean. An emperor penguin has powerful wings. It uses its wings as flippers while it swims. Its body is **streamlined**, or smoothly shaped, allowing the penguin to swim quickly through water. An emperor penguin must swim quickly to find food and avoid **predators**. Predators are animals that hunt and eat other animals.

An emperor penguin can see well both in water and on land.

Feathers cover and protect an emperor penguin's ears. The penguin has good hearing, however.

An emperor penguin cannot fly because its wings are too small to lift its heavy body off the ground.

An emperor penguin's beak has nostrils that are suited to cold weather. When the penguin breathes out, its nostrils are warmed by the breath. When it breathes in, the cold air is warmed by the penguin's nostrils.

*A thick, feathered flap of skin hangs from an emperor penguin's belly. The skin is called a **brood pouch**.*

Strong claws help an emperor penguin grip slippery ice while it walks.

*An emperor penguin uses its **webbed feet** to steer and stop in water.*

Feathers and fat

An emperor penguin has two layers of feathers that keep its body warm. The outer layer of feathers is made up of many small feathers, which are covered in oil. The oil makes the feathers **waterproof**. Under the layer of small feathers, the penguin has a layer of warm, fluffy feathers called **down**. Down traps warm air close to the penguin's skin. Under its skin, a penguin has a thick layer of **blubber**, or fat, that also helps keep the penguin warm. In fact, with all its layers, the penguin sometimes gets too hot! To cool off, the penguin fluffs up its feathers or spreads its wings to release body heat.

Dressed for success

Penguins have white bellies and black backs. This contrast in colors is called **countershading**. Countershading is coloring that makes it difficult for predators to see an animal. When a penguin swims above a predator, the predator may not notice it because the penguin's white belly blends in with the bright water above. When a penguin swims below a predator, the predator may not notice it because the penguin's black back blends in with the dark water below.

What is a life cycle?

Every animal goes through a set of changes as it grows. These changes are called a **life cycle**. Early in an animal's life cycle, the animal is born or hatches from an egg. The animal grows and changes until it is **mature**, or an adult. A mature animal can **mate**, or join with another animal of its species to make babies.

Life span

A life cycle is not the same as a **life span**. An animal's life span is the length of time the animal lives. Despite its harsh habitat, an emperor penguin has a life span of about 20 years. Some emperor penguins live to be 40 years old!

An emperor penguin's life cycle

An emperor penguin begins its life cycle as an **embryo**, or developing baby, inside an egg laid by its mother. The egg is **incubated**, or kept warm, by the father. While the egg is being incubated, the embryo develops. When the egg has been incubated for about 64 days, a **chick** hatches from the egg. A chick is a baby bird. The chick's mother and father take turns feeding it, keeping it warm, and protecting it from predators. When the chick is five months old, its parents no longer take care of it. Soon the chick **molts**, or sheds, its feathers and grows new ones. After it molts, the young penguin is called a **fledgling**. The fledgling continues to grow and develop until it is mature. A female emperor penguin is mature when it is five years old. A male emperor penguin is mature when it is five to six years old.

mature emperor penguin

egg

newly hatched chick

one-month-old chick

five-month-old fledgling

Journey on the ice

Colonies of emperor penguins live mainly in the ocean. When winter begins, they move onto pack ice to lay their eggs and raise their chicks. On the ice, a colony travels from 31 to 75 miles (50-121 km) to reach its **breeding ground**. A breeding ground is the area where a colony of penguins mates and lays eggs. The penguins travel for days by walking or **tobogganing**. Penguins toboggan by sliding on their bellies, using their wings and feet to push themselves along.

No food for the journey

Emperor penguins do not eat any food from the time they leave the ocean until they return to it. While they are on pack ice, penguins live off their blubber. Blubber provides them with the energy they need to survive. Penguins also do not drink water on the pack ice. They eat snow to get the water they need to survive.

For penguins, tobogganing is faster than walking!

Penguin party

A colony of penguins reaches its breeding ground by May. Most breeding grounds are in sheltered areas on the pack ice, where large **ice cliffs**, or steep walls of ice, help protect the penguins from strong winds.

The colony of penguins in its breeding ground is called a **rookery**. Some rookeries are small, whereas others are large. There may be as many as 40,000 emperor penguins in a single rookery!

Penguin partners

Male emperor penguins arrive at the breeding ground shortly before females do. When female penguins reach the breeding ground, each male penguin puts on a **display**, or pattern of behavior, to attract a female. A male puts on a display by standing still, letting his head fall to his chest, and loudly **trumpeting**. A penguin trumpets by calling out to another penguin. If a female accepts the male, she loudly trumpets back to him. The male and female become **partners**. Partners are two penguins that mate with each other.

These partners are trumpeting to each other.

Learning the calls

After mating, the partners live together in the rookery. They stand together, trumpeting to each other over and over. Each penguin has its own call. The partners keep trumpeting in order to learn what each other's call sounds like.

One egg only

About 45 days after mating, the female penguin lays one large, greenish-white egg. She lays the egg onto her own feet! Most birds build nests in which to lay their eggs. Emperor penguins cannot build nests for their eggs. There are no sticks or grass for building nests—only snow and ice.

*A pair of penguins forms a special **bond**. The penguins do not mate with other penguins. Their bond helps them work together to raise their chick during the harsh Antarctic winter.*

The emperors and the eggs

Soon after a mother lays an egg, she passes it to the father penguin. To pass the egg, the mother gently rolls it from her feet onto the father's feet. Both penguins must be extremely careful while they pass the egg. If the egg is on the ice for longer than a few seconds, it will crack. If the egg cracks, the embryo inside the egg dies.

Back to the ocean

Once the egg is safely on the father's feet, the mother penguin returns to the ocean to find food. She used up a lot of her blubber carrying and laying the egg. She must build up more blubber so she can survive the winter.

Mother penguins may keep the eggs for several hours before passing them to the fathers. The eggs are fragile, and passing them is risky.

Warming the egg

A father penguin incubates the egg for the rest of the winter. The father balances the egg on his feet and covers it with his thick brood pouch to keep it warm. The brood pouch protects the egg from freezing temperatures and harsh winds.

Huddle up!

Since father penguins have no food to eat, they must **conserve**, or save, energy while they incubate the eggs. They conserve energy by standing still and by sleeping for long periods of time. To stay warm, the father penguins **huddle** together.

These father penguins are huddling to stay warm.

17

The chicks hatch

In early July, the chicks hatch from their eggs. The chicks have black heads with white patches around their eyes and cheeks. They are covered with downy, gray feathers. Chicks are about six inches (15 cm) tall and weigh about 11 ounces (312 g).

Hungry chicks

Newly hatched chicks are helpless. Father penguins must feed their chicks and keep them warm.

As soon as a chick hatches, it whistles to ask for food. The father penguin **regurgitates**, or brings up, a milky liquid into his beak and feeds it to the chick. The liquid comes from a pouch deep in his throat. The father has only enough food to feed the chick for a short time, however.

Newly hatched penguin chicks do not have blubber or thick feathers. They come out of the brood pouch only to eat.

The mothers return

Mother penguins leave the ocean and return to the rookery soon after the chicks hatch. Scientists are not sure how mother penguins know when to make the trip back to their rookeries. A mother penguin finds her family among all the other penguins in the rookery by trumpeting loudly. She listens for her partner to return her call. The mother and father continue to trumpet back and forth until they find each other.

These mother penguins are on their way back to their rookery. The food they found in the ocean has given them enough energy to make their trip.

Chick care

When a father and a mother penguin find each other, the father passes the chick quickly from his pouch to her pouch. This is a dangerous time for the chick. If the chick stays on the ice for too long, it freezes to death. Once the chick is safely in the mother's pouch, the father returns to the ocean to eat. By this time, the father has not eaten for about three months. He has used up nearly half of his blubber. Father penguins may have to walk for days to reach the ocean before they can eat.

A newly hatched chick can survive on the ice for about two minutes. It is important to pass the chick quickly.

Mom's turn

A mother penguin cares for the chick by keeping it in her brood pouch. She regurgitates food for the chick. After feeding in the ocean for two months, the mother penguin has plenty of food for the chick.

Sharing the care

For two to three weeks, the father penguin feeds in the ocean. He then returns to help take care of the chick again. Each parent takes a turn feeding the chick and protecting it from predators, while the other parent returns to the ocean to feed. The parents must eat often to survive the winter and provide enough food for their chick to survive. The chick grows quickly!

Chirping chicks

A chick chirps constantly. Its chirp is different than the chirp of any other chick. Each parent learns its chick's call. When a parent returns from the ocean to feed its chick, it listens for its chick's call. It feeds only its own chick.

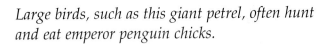

Large birds, such as this giant petrel, often hunt and eat emperor penguin chicks.

Growing in a group

When a chick is about two months old, it is too big to fit inside a brood pouch. It gathers together with other chicks in a large group called a **crèche**. The chicks in a crèche huddle together to stay warm. Although the chick's parents no longer protect it, both the mother and father penguins continue to feed the chick. The parents travel to the ocean often to eat and bring back food for the chick. The chick needs a steady supply of food to grow and to keep enough blubber on its body to stay warm.

A two-month-old emperor-penguin chick weighs about four pounds (2 kg).

On its own

When a chick is about five months old, it is half the size of a mature penguin. Its mother and father now stop feeding it, so the chick has to find food on its own. The parents leave the chick and return to live in the ocean. The chick soon goes to live in the ocean, as well.

New feathers

The chick travels with other chicks to the ocean to begin searching for food. The young chick must molt before it can swim in the icy waters, however. As the chick walks toward the ocean, it begins to lose its fluffy down. It grows the oily, waterproof feathers it needs to survive in water. By the time the chick reaches the ocean, it has grown its waterproof feathers. It is now a fledgling. Fledgling penguins first swim in the ocean during summer. They enter the freezing water in small groups and know by **instinct** how to swim, dive, and find food.

Chicks eat a lot and grow quickly.

23

Mature penguins

Fledglings enter the Southern Ocean for the first time in summer. There is more food in the Southern Ocean in summer than there is at any other time of the year. Fledglings swim many miles out in the ocean to eat.

The cycle continues

Most fledglings make their first trips to the breeding grounds when they are four. They are not yet mature and do not mate on their first trips, however. When emperor penguins are five or six years old, they are mature. They travel to their breeding grounds to mate with other mature penguins and care for their chicks. After feeding and protecting their chicks for about five months, the adults return to the ocean.

These mature penguins are returning to the ocean.

Molting

Mature emperor penguins spend about one month in the ocean finding food and putting on the blubber they lost during the winter. Then they move onto pack ice to molt. Mature penguins molt for about three to four weeks. They cannot enter the water until their feathers have grown back, so they do not eat again until they finish molting.

Emperor penguins lose their old, worn-out feathers in large patches.

Preening penguins

Whether they are in water or on ice, emperor penguins **preen** often. Preening is cleaning, combing, and oiling feathers. Penguins use their beaks to comb their feathers into place. Then they take oil from body parts called **preen glands**, which are located near their tails, and spread the oil over their feathers. The oil makes the feathers smooth, shiny, and waterproof. Preened feathers help keep penguins warm and allow them to move smoothly through water.

Life in the ocean

A penguin's mouth

A penguin has no teeth. Instead, its mouth and tongue are lined with sharp, backward-pointing spines. The spines help the penguin hold on to food, which it swallows whole.

Emperor penguins are **carnivores**, or animals that eat other animals. They eat mainly shrimplike animals called krill. They also eat fish and squid. Emperor penguins use their sharp beaks to catch **prey**. Prey are animals that predators hunt.

Penguin predators

Leopard seals and orcas are animals that hunt and eat emperor penguins. To escape from these predators, penguins swim and dive quickly in the water. They may also leap out of the water onto pack ice.

leopard seal

This penguin is escaping a predator.

Deep-sea divers

Emperor penguins are better divers than are any other species of bird. They dive quickly and deeply to catch prey. A mature emperor penguin may dive for prey as many as a hundred times a day. They can dive as deep as 1,300 to 1,475 feet (396-450 m). Some emperor penguins can even hold their breath for up to 20 minutes!

Some of these penguins are hunting. Others are swimming to the surface for air.

Long live the emperors!

Scientists estimate that there are about 400,000 to 450,000 emperor penguins living in the Southern Ocean. Emperor penguins are not currently **endangered**, or at risk of dying out in the **wild**.

The main reason that emperor penguins are not endangered is that they live far away from people. The actions of people around the world can harm emperor penguins, however.

People hurting penguins

People used to hunt penguins for their blubber, which they used to make oil for lamps. They also gathered and ate penguin eggs. It is now against the law to gather penguin eggs or to hunt penguins. Some **commercial fisheries** continue to catch krill, fish, and other animals in the Southern Ocean, however. Commercial fisheries are businesses that catch and sell fish. If commercial fisheries **overfish** the animals penguins hunt, penguins may not have enough food to eat. Some penguins also get caught and tangled in fishing nets. They cannot get to the water's surface for air, and they die.

Global warming

One of the biggest threats to emperor penguins is **global warming**. Global warming is a rise in the average temperature of Earth. It occurs when **greenhouse gases** are released into air. Global warming results in less pack ice around Antarctica on which penguins can lay their eggs and raise their chicks. Soon the penguins will have nowhere to lay their eggs.

Melting before molting

Emperor penguins lay their eggs far from water. This distance gives chicks time to molt before the pack ice starts to melt. Global warming causes pack ice to melt and break up earlier than it should. If pack ice melts too early, ocean water reaches chicks before they have molted. Without their waterproof feathers, the chicks drown or freeze to death in the ocean.

Global warming destroys the Antarctic habitat.

People and penguins

Some scientists study penguins in the wild. The scientists live and work in research stations in Antarctica. By studying penguins, scientists learn more about these amazing birds and how they survive in the Antarctic climate. There are currently about 45 research stations in Antarctica. In summer, about 4,000 people live at the research stations. In winter, about 1,000 people live there.

The Antarctic Treaty
The Antarctic Treaty protects all the wildlife in Antarctica. It is a document that has been signed by the governments of 45 countries. The treaty prevents people from harming the Antarctic habitat or wildlife.

The Argentina Research Station is in Antarctica. There are currently about 45 other research stations in Antarctica.

Tourism

Each year, the number of tourists visiting Antarctica during the summer months increases. Once tourists see emperor penguins and the habitat in which they live, they understand why Antarctica is so special and why people should protect it. These people can help educate other people about the threats that emperor penguins face. Tourists must be careful to avoid disturbing emperor penguins or polluting their habitat, however.

Learn more

You do not need to visit Antarctica to learn about penguins! Visit your local library to find other books, DVDs, and resources about emperor penguins. You can also watch the movie *March of the Penguins* or waddle on to these websites for fun facts, photographs, and more.

www.nationalgeographic.com/kids/creature_feature/0101/penguins.html
www.nationalgeographic.com/xpeditions/activities/10/mpenguins1.html
www.enchantedlearning.com/school/Antarctica/

Glossary

Note: Boldfaced words that are defined in the text may not appear in the glossary.

bond An emotion or interest that is shared

climate The long-term weather conditions in an area

continent One of the seven large areas of land on Earth (Africa, Antarctica, Asia, Australia, Europe, North America, and South America)

greenhouse gases Dangerous gases in air that contribute to global warming

huddle To stand in a group

instinct A natural awareness that controls animal behaviors

overfish To remove too many fish from a habitat

precipitation Water that falls from the sky, such as snow or rain

Southern Hemisphere The southern half of Earth

waterproof Describing something that is resistant to water

webbed feet Describing feet with thin sheets of skin between the toes

wild Natural areas not controlled by people

Index

blubber 9, 12, 16, 18, 20, 22, 25, 28
bodies 4, 8-9, 22, 25
breeding ground 12, 13, 14, 24
brood pouch 8, 17, 18, 20, 21, 22
chicks 11, 12, 15, 18, 19, 20-23, 24, 29

colonies 5, 7, 12, 13
eggs 10, 11, 12, 15, 16-17, 18, 28, 29
embryo 11, 16
feathers 4, 5, 8, 9, 11, 18, 23, 25, 29
fledgling 11, 23, 24
food 5, 8, 12, 16, 17, 18, 19, 21, 22, 23, 24, 25, 26, 28

hatching 10, 11, 18, 19, 20
mating 10, 12, 14, 15, 24
mature 10, 11, 23, 24-25, 27
molting 11, 23, 25, 29
pack ice 6, 12, 13, 25, 26, 29
rookeries 13, 15, 19
swimming 4, 6, 8, 9, 23, 24, 26, 27
trumpeting 14, 15, 19

1 2 3 4 5 6 7 8 9 0 Printed in the U.S.A. 5 4 3 2 1 0 9 8 7 6